Building a Marriage

Building a Marriage

Ten Tools for Creating, Repairing, and Maintaining Your Lives Together

CRANOR F. GRAVES

New York

Library of Congress Cataloging-in-Publication Data
Graves, Cranor F.
Building a marriage: ten tools for creating, repairing, and maintaining your lives together / Cranor F. Graves.—1st ed.
p. cm.
ISBN 1-56282-958-0
1. Marriage—United States. 2. Communication in marriage—United States.   I. Title.
HQ734.G725   1993
646.7′8—dc20
                                                                                93-15725
                                                                                CIP

Design by Irva Mandelbaum

First Edition
10 9 8 7 6 5 4 3 2 1

To Rita

Every couple I have counseled has contributed something to this book; many have read chapters and made helpful suggestions.

In particular, I thank Kathy Theden for processing my words and Jane M. Harvey for encouraging me to write them.

Thanks to Rhoda Weyr, my agent.

CONTENTS

Contents

◯◯　x　◯◯

INTRODUCTION

This is a plain book for people who want their marriage to grow. It is also for people entering marriage who want their optimism to have a realistic foundation. In our society there isn't much preparation for marriage; in fact, you have to be more knowledgeable and responsible to get a driver's license than to get a marriage license.

The American myth is that a wedding is a marriage. The myth implies that after the wedding ceremony the relationship goes on automatic pilot, just flies without further attention from either spouse. Then when problems do arise, as they inevitably will, we decide we must have married the wrong person. Then we may go off and find another partner instead of learning something from the first experience.

This book is not intended to put marriage counselors out of business. Some couples may even need marriage counseling in order to prepare themselves to use this book to full advantage. The purpose of this book is to give two good people ten good tools to keep their marriage in good repair.

Marriage can be destructive to the partners or marriage can be a good experience in which two people learn to know and like themselves and each other and together grow as human beings.

In this manual I talk a lot about my own marriage, for two reasons. First, it is the marriage I know best, although as a marriage counselor I have come to know many others. Second, it is the marriage I most admire and from which I have learned more than from books, workshops, conferences, and marriage therapy sessions with others.

No two good and rewarding marriages are alike. Each one is a growing and changing relationship between two unique people. But there are basic tools for building, maintaining, and frequently remodeling a marriage so that the marriage experience continually encourages the partners to keep working at it. That work may seem to be the hardest work in the world, but it can also be the most rewarding for two people who undertake it with these ten basic tools.

We know what won't work. We've tried it over and over and over again. Our tendency is to go on trying what won't work, saying it louder, trying it harder. Instead of repeating what won't work, let's try something else. Let's take these ten tools and learn how to use them. Good tools work well when we use them with skill. When we don't use them, even the best tools only gather dust.

I call these chapters *tools;* they are attitudes, stances, points of view, values that help to maintain and, when needed, repair a relationship.

Sometimes we spend more energy working on the house and the car than we do in caring for the relationship. We have a schedule for cleaning the house; we repair what's broken. We clean and oil a hunting rifle or golf clubs; we wash and wax a car; we mow the lawn. We work hard to keep *things* in good condition. In short, when we have something worth keeping, we take care of it. Apply this theme to marriage.

These tools are as different from one another as are a hammer, pliers, wrench, or measuring tape. What these tools do have in common is that they are simple, basic, effective. There are surely other tools, but this is the basic tool kit.

People marry with good will and optimism, even if it's the third marriage after the second divorce. There is a built-in optimism: "This time, this one is *it!*" And more people would make a go of marriage if they knew how, had the tools. Here, then, are ten tools to make the marriage "run right," to make it purr like a kitten, to make it spin and hum like a top.

Building a Marriage

The First Tool

FORTHRIGHTNESS

What we all want is:
>a person I can trust
>>who will also trust me,
>a person who will tell me the truth
>>who will also believe me,
>a person who will level with me
>>who will also listen to me,
>a person I can believe in
>>who will also believe in me.

All these qualities relate to forthrightness, the first of ten tools that not only maintain and repair a marriage daily but also work to bond a couple in the comfort of a love that grows deeper and stronger as the years go on.

Here are some options. As my partner in marriage, you will know what I think, how I feel, and what I want because:

(a) People who really love each other just know these things about the person they love.

(b) Husbands and wives are clairvoyant.

(c) I'll tell you.

And as your partner in marriage, I'll know what you think, feel, and want because:

(a) You'll drop plenty of hints.
(b) If I love you enough, those things about you will become obvious to me.
(c) You'll tell me.

When two people make an agreement to choose answer (c) and abide by the terms of it, they will reveal to each other their thoughts, their feelings, and their desires. Only then will the air clear from the smoke of confusion that results from guessing, mind reading, and presuming.

> **You will know what I want,**
> **you will know what I feel,**
> **you will know what I think,**
> **because I will tell you.**

This agreement applies to all those things that affect and are important to the relationship. There is still room for some privacy: For example, I don't need to know what my wife is thinking when she is watching Robert Redford. Each partner maintains a right to privacy because being married does not mean that one stops being an individual. Having to explain or account for every moment, every penny, every thought, would be a burdensome violation of privacy. Excessive accountability is contrary to the atmosphere of mutual trust.

Updating

For the most part, however, we have to make clear what's happening inside us when our thinking and feeling and wanting affect the marriage. And because we are all changing human beings, we need to bring each other up to date and make known the changes we have experienced. Otherwise, we find ourselves responding in terms of something that was said six months ago, perhaps in a bad moment. What was true then may not be true now.

> "But you don't like broccoli!"
> "Well, yes, I've learned to like it at the cafeteria at work; I eat it often now."
>
> "But you always said you had no interest in sports."
> "True, but I do like to watch the NCAA finals."

Correcting and updating is hard work. However, short of reading each other's mind, it's the only way for growing, changing people to relate to each other as they are at the present moment.

Another good reason for announcing what's going on inside us is that our mates may interpret silence or withdrawal as anger or punishment. Forthrightness intervenes and corrects misperceptions: "I love you. I am not rejecting you. And I need a few hours alone." In other words, when I need quiet, space, or time apart, I will announce it; *I will tell you* clearly what I want.

When I was talking about this issue with Henry and Ruth, a couple in their early twenties, Ruth said, "If I have to ask for what I want, it takes all the pleasure away." I didn't agree. When I say, "Please pass the salt and pepper," is my seasoned food less tasty to me because no one anticipated my desire for salt and pepper?

Ruth was able to agree that, in essence, she was expressing the myth that lovers are psychic: If you loved me, you'd know me well enough to anticipate what I want.

Guessing, hinting, and mind reading are poor substitutes for genuine communication between two people. The love and intimacy of marriage do not result in partners growing antennae able to receive signals and keep the couple tuned in and in tune. True, people who know each other well can sometimes anticipate each other's responses; but to know even each other's tastes, preferences, and pet peeves, much less each other's dreams, desires, fears, thoughts, and feelings, requires talking: telling, listening, sharing, verbalizing, articulating, conversing, pillow-talk—call it what you will, but do it.

Be frank. Be forthright. Why couch an important message to an important person in chitchat? Why use vague, roundabout examples to illustrate the point? Why play guessing games for the sake of "being nice"? Here's a well-meant but exasperating dialogue:

"Would you like to go out for supper tonight?"
"Oh, I don't know; would you?"
"Whatever you'd like is fine with me."
"Well, where would you like to go?"
"I don't know; where would *you* like to go?"

Neither partner has revealed even a hint of self, an opinion, a preference, or a truth. What does this game of verbal Ping-Pong reveal? Neither partner wants to risk a no or to take responsibility for the choice.

A no to a suggestion is not a rejection of the person making that suggestion. Why, then, is the risk so threatening? True, when I tell you what I want, I make myself vulnerable. Then reassure me that your no is not a rejection of me; it's just that you don't care to do what I have proposed.

Forthrightness is a tool requiring two operators as certainly as a crosscut saw requires two operators. If one is free to make a suggestion and the other is not free to make a countersuggestion, we end up with a director and a doormat.

Try It

When I ask a couple to foresee potential problems with the forthrightness tool, the most frequent response is that one person could be too blunt and hurt the other's feelings. The second most frequent response is that one could dominate the other by always expressing what he or she wants. True, forthrightness must be tempered by diplomacy, tact, and thoughtfulness. But the advantage of forthrightness outweighs the disadvantage. As long as I remember the safeguard of my wife's right to also respond forthrightly, there is little danger of abuse. Each of us can suggest; each of us can say, "Yes, thank you" or "No, thank you." Try it. You'll see how hard it is to carry out but also how rewarding it can be to you both.

I'm suggesting that we can cut through a lot of cotton candy by saying, "I would like . . ." with clear understanding that our partner is equally free to respond. Since we don't own each other, we cannot always expect a positive response to what we would prefer, but I assure you that you will get what you want more often by stating what you want than by wishing or by waiting for somebody else to fulfill your needs and desires.

Couples who come for marriage counseling often spend the early sessions telling me what their spouses think. Gradually they learn to speak for themselves and to listen when the other speaks for himself or herself.

When a wife guesses what her husband thinks, her guess becomes her real perception. Unless the guesswork is corrected, she'll act on that perception, which to her is reality—the way he does think, in her mind. Let me give you an example: My wife says she would like for us to spend twenty dollars on a gift for our friend's birthday (good forthrightness there). I do not answer at once, because I'm pondering it. She interprets my silence as a negative response.

What I wish I had done was to say at once, "Let me think about it for a moment, and then I'll respond."

When a husband decides in advance what his wife's reaction will be ("I know what she'd say"), his decision about her attitude is as real to him as if she had actually said it. Then each one reacts to what he or she presumes to be the other's position or stance. That's mind reading, and it is no substitute for talking and listening in turn. And it leads to resentment.

The joke about the man who has a flat tire in the country at midnight illustrates reacting to presumptions. When the man opens his trunk, there's no jack. He looks up and down the road, and sees a dim light in the distance. "Ah, a farmer's house! I'll walk over there, borrow his jack, change my tire, and be on my way." As he walks toward the light, he begins having second thoughts: "Man, it's really late, and that farmer isn't going to appreciate being waked up at midnight!" As he turns into the farmer's lane, the farmer's dogs begin to bark. His apprehension mounts. "What if he thinks I've come to rob him? What if he sics his dogs on me? What if he comes to the door angry and with his shotgun?" As his anxiety level increases, he reaches the front door and knocks. In a short time the farmer comes to the door and says, "What can I do for you?" With his fear still rising, all the man can say is, "You can *keep* your damned jack!" So it goes when we decide in advance how the other person will probably react.

A Test

A good test of how well we communicate with and understand each other is to ask each spouse: "How do you know when your partner is angry?" The desirable answer is "I know when he is angry because he tells me so, and he tells me what he is angry about." However, the typical answer is "He clams up." "She withdraws into monosyllables." "He pouts." "She slams doors." Each one of the above is a variation on a theme of noncommunication or very inadequate communication, which leads to more frustration and confusion and misunderstanding and guessing and hurt and anger.

All of this is to say: We have to *tell each other* what's happening. One evening I raced home for supper between appointments to find my wife preoccupied, distant, withdrawn. I perceived that she didn't want me there, although it was she who had suggested that I come home for supper instead of grabbing a bite downtown. My perception was my reality until my wife corrected that perception. "Bear with me," she said. "This has been a terrible day at work. I'm not rejecting you; I just feel very tired and depressed."

That forthright statement helped me understand the reason for her emotional distance, she wasn't rejecting me; she didn't resent my presence. She was hurting. I started toward her to embrace her, to comfort her. My new perception was that to hug her would help. "Please don't," she said—still another clear message for me. I kept a respectful distance. I now knew that acceding to her wishes was the only constructive action I could take. We sat down for supper as friends; we both understood that she wanted to deal with her depression alone.

By the time I returned home from my night appointments, my wife had put the dishes in the dishwasher, curled up under an afghan with the evening paper, and all was well. If she had said nothing before supper, I would have reacted on the basis of that perception—my reality—and felt rejected and angry: "She asked me to come home for supper, and now she wishes I hadn't come. And I have driven all the way across town just to have supper with her!" Had she not corrected my second perception that my comforting arms were the cure, I would have reacted on that perception and imposed on her an inappropriate, perhaps smothering (although well-meant) gesture.

Nice Guys Can Say No

Clare and Edward believed they had a basically good marriage. However, there was some unidentified sore spot that was festering. They couldn't identify the sore spot until they began working with this tool of forthrightness. They came to see that their real problem was rooted in the most central issue in a marriage: how to balance the healthy interdependence of two people with the necessary independence of each individual.

It worked out like this: Their last fight was over Edward's having committed himself to help a friend wire his home, a commitment that would involve six Saturdays in a row. Clare resented this time "stolen" from her and the children. I pointed out that Clare was paying Edward a compliment, because some wives would be delighted to be rid of their husbands for six Saturdays.

We could all feel the tension rising in the room. Finally Edward said,

"Clare, I feel that most of the time when we're doing things together, I'm your escort; we're doing things I don't especially like because you want to do them. I resent always going along. I need to do things for me sometimes. I'll enjoy helping my friend Dave wire his house."

Together, the three of us discovered issues that involve two of our ten tools at once. First, Edward was seeing Clare as the dominant partner who planned things for them to do, and he felt the need to dig in his heels once in a while to preserve his own identity. Edward was a considerate man, sensitive to the family's needs; but his desire to please Clare overwhelmed him. The balance needed was the forthrightness to say no on occasion instead of always going along with Clare's plans like a good guy.

This was their pattern: Clare made suggestions; Edward said yes even when he really wanted to say no. The twofold result: Clare accepted his yes as his truthful answer. Edward went along in his role as escort, filled with resentment.

When Edward came to realize that nice guys *can* say no, that a husband doesn't exist only to please his wife, that he was free to negotiate, then good things began to happen—good things like trusting a mutual yes as authentic; good things like accepting disagreement without feeling rejection.

When forthrightness freed each of them to say yes or no honestly to each other's suggestions, a new level of trust grew between them. When one of them suggested a family picnic and the other accepted the suggestion, both of them knew the agreement was genuine. They learned that a response of no to a suggestion is not at all the same as rejecting the person.

It didn't come easily, this new level of forthrightness. When a man or a woman has been a pleaser for years, he or she has to work hard to balance that admirable trait with the degree of healthy independence that justifies an occasional "no, thank you."

To achieve forthrightness, then, we make a simple contract (easy to make, hard to carry out, rewarding when done):

> **We agree to tell each other what we think,**
> **what we want,**
> **what we feel—about**
> **whatever**
> **concerns**
> **us.**

And we agree to respect each other's right to say yes or no or to offer a countersuggestion.

There is still room for generosity. When my wife wants to visit relatives, and my yes stretches my generosity, it is still my choice; and my genuine yes does not carry with it the price tag of pouting or resentment. I have chosen freely and generously.

Our goal in making this simple contract is to avoid second-guessing, to overcome the habit of interpreting words and events negatively, to stop trying to read each other's mind. Our goal is not to reveal everything we think or want or feel or fantasize but only to reveal clearly whatever concerns our relationship.

Our goal is to speak our minds and to respond with a frank answer that can be trusted as true.

The Second Tool

CONFLICT

Where did we ever get the idea that there is to be no pain in a good relationship? Who taught us to try to avoid pain by running from conflict? Aren't we bound to get on each other's nerves occasionally? Aren't we likely to do things that annoy each other? Aren't our preferences going to conflict sometimes? Pain is a part of life.

In marriage, the choice is between the constructive pain of dealing with conflict or the destructive pain of running away from it; the constructive pain when we deal with issues or the destructive pain when we ignore them.

Our goal is not always to avoid pain. In fact, we sometimes choose pain because we determine the pain to be helpful. We elect to go to the dentist with a decaying tooth because not to go would be both painful and destructive. To go to the dentist is to invite constructive pain.

When my wife says or does something that annoys me, I have the choice of telling her (constructive pain, as we deal with the issue) or keeping my resentment inside (destructive pain). And what happens when it festers? A degree of emotional divorce is what happens. A distance widens between us until one of us has the generous courage to broach the issue.

When couples report to me that they never have conflicts, I feel regret. Is one of them not thinking? Do they never disagree because they are keeping it all inside? Are they sweeping everything under the rug? How dull their life must be, how removed from each other their cohabiting must be.

Conflict is not only inevitable, it is also desirable. There will eventually be conflict between two people who think and feel. If each will listen to the other, both will learn something. I grant that in the very early stages of a relationship there may be no conflict. At first we are amazed and delighted at how much we have in common: tastes, interests, preferences. Sooner or later, though, we reach some point of conflict. No two people (unless one is a clone of the other) can possibly agree on everything. Nor should they try to.

If a bride and groom think that their marriage will go well "naturally" just because they love each other, they are believing a cultural myth. This widely accepted myth tells two people that they were made for each other, that just as a young swan takes to the water and swims by instinct when it hits water, so their relationship will proceed swimmingly, by instinct, without thought or effort, because they have married. The myth says that since marriages ought to go well naturally, there must be something wrong with the people who have conflicts. Consequently, they are reluctant to admit, even to themselves, at first, that they have problems. Then, it seems difficult to seek help because that implies failure. When conflicts arise—conflicts that are part of every growing and healthy relationship—each partner may wonder if perhaps he or she married the wrong person. Instead of questioning the myth, they question the marriage. What a paralyzing myth!

One of the first steps toward exploding the myth that a good relationship always runs smoothly is to accept the fact, as soon as it becomes evident, that couples do not have built-in, instinctive equipment to make a marriage work.

To put it another way, conflicts don't mean that something is wrong with the marriage. Conflicts only mean that two people are thinking and feeling and expressing themselves honestly. That's all.

Two Winners

The purpose of facing conflict is not to win or lose. In fact, we have two winners and no losers when we discuss our differences and the reasons for them and when we both accept the better opinion, no matter who holds it. On the other hand, we will have two losers and no winners if both talk and neither listens. This is destructive pain. Call it interrupted monologue.

I use the word "conflict" because to some people "fighting" is a dirty word. Conflict simply means that two opinions are meeting each other. There will be no conflict, ever, if one spouse turns his or her brain to off; but what a loss! No one person knows everything, and every person knows something. The message is this: Share what little we know so that both of us may be richer.

The truth is that healthy people have conflict, and they always will. Each spouse changes and grows, or wants to grow. Circumstances change. And some conflict is inevitable, as it is in every type of close relationship.

My wife knew this before I did, and I learned from her. Once, in the first year of our marriage, we were having a heated discussion (conflict). I felt threatened. Finally, I said, "Do you want a divorce?" She answered, "No! I want to fight!" To her, the deep bond between us was in no way threatened by the fight that was occurring on the surface. She has taught me that it is safe to express our differing views when both are honest and willing to listen in turn.

Name the Enemy

It is also important to identify the enemy accurately. The enemy is not the other person. The enemy is withdrawal. The enemy is a breakdown in communication that can only lead to mind reading, an art whose state is nowhere. The enemy is nursing bruises instead of healing them. The enemy is not listening.

Phyllis McGinley said it well:

Sticks and stones are hard on bones.
Aimed with deadly art,
Words can sting like anything.
But silence breaks the heart.

Put it another way: if we don't tell each other what we think and how we feel, we'll have to guess. And too frequently we guess wrong, don't we?

When I seek to avoid the pain of conflict, by withdrawing into pouting solitude, that is just the catch: I sentence myself to solitary confinement. Who is punished?

Now it can happen that we are not quite ready to talk to each other. We are too hurt, too angry, too sure that one is right and the other wrong. We may take one of two paths:

(a) We may seek out a therapist if we cannot hear each other. Therapists will not act as judge and jury. Their function is not to take sides or to find the guilty party. Their function is to interpret, to translate, to help partners hear each other, evaluate, negotiate.

(b) One of us may choose to lean on a friend's shoulder first. Talking with a friend cannot be the last step of the path, although talking to a trusted friend first is good if we keep in mind that a friend is hearing only one side.

In either case, talking to a third party, friend or therapist, is no substitute for talking—and listening—to each other. The third party is the means to the end.

After a cooling-off period, we remind ourselves that we did not come together for the purpose of making each other miserable. We came together to be friends and lovers, to be good for each other. And friends and lovers are good listeners.

"It's Not Nice to Be Angry"

As I grew up, my family had the unspoken understanding that we were to avoid conflict at all costs. We went around "being nice" to one another. Instead of seeing differences as legitimate, instead of seeing anger as an essential emotion, we looked upon these feelings as somehow unworthy of decent people. Now I know that trying to avoid anger is like trying to avoid being sleepy or hungry.

When anger is expressed respectfully, hot and clean, not by attacking or name calling, the anger goes away. Anger not dealt with does not go away, except in the translated form of headaches and ulcers, sarcasm and depression, and emotional distance and resentment. We are not as fragile as we might think. Yet how long a list of reasons we draw up for not dealing openly with conflict:

"Things are going pretty well right now; I don't want to rock the
    boat."
"I don't want to hurt your feelings."
"You couldn't take it."
"I'm not willing to risk your anger."
"I don't want to burden you with my problems."
"I'll lose your love if we disagree."
"It's no use trying. I know what you'd say."

That last one is a lulu! Translate it. It means that I can read your mind.
And it's not fair. Even if you have reacted the same way to the same situation
for the last umpteen times, what right have I to say that you can't grow or
change or have a new opinion? Why, today could be the very day that you
come back with a new response!

I can think of only one other reason for not dealing openly and honestly
with feelings that is more disrespectful than the last one above: the assump-
tion that "You wouldn't listen because you don't care."

When I find myself getting angry in our relationship, I can usually trace
it back to my not having spoken up soon enough about something that was
bothering me. Today, I'm going to make a resolution: "Never for the sake of
so-called peace and quiet will I deny my own experience and convictions."
And remember, too: A person who can understand and integrate his anger as
part of himself will not become violent.

Humor

A sense of humor helps. In our marriage, we have a joke: "There are only two
ways of doing something—my way and the wrong way." That fits both of us

and helps us avoid taking ourselves too seriously and with such deadly earnestness. Nowadays, we can have a good laugh when we make the bed together in the morning, even though each one of us has a set notion about how to make a bed.

"We've been married for forty years and never had a disagreement" is hardly a model for marriage. To me, it means either that the couple is lying; or that they no longer care enough about each other or their marriage to share their thoughts, feelings, desires, opinions; or that one of them does the thinking for the two of them. None of these possibilities are acceptable. Conflict means dealing with the issues. It is only when issues are not dealt with that they become problems. So many people are taught that there are good feelings, which are acceptable, and bad feelings, which are unacceptable. The truth is that there *are* feelings. Some feel good; some feel bad. The point is, the feelings are there. We have feelings.

A bad feeling is a signal that something needs to be done. A good feeling is a signal that something needs to be enjoyed.

Name the Goal

Why don't we learn to take every conflict that occurs as an invitation to ask, "What is the goal? What is the goal in this discussion?" All conflict revolves around one of two issues: the truth or the common good.

Truth: Is the sofa we both like too long for the space between our living room windows?

We're shopping for a new sofa. We find one we both like in the third furniture store we visit. The question of length arises: Will it fit our space? I think it will fit; my wife thinks it's too long. This is a conflict that could stall in an argument, "It will fit." "It won't." But why not get a yardstick and arrive at the truth? Whatever the truth is, we end up with two winners. After all, neither of us wants to make the wrong purchase.

The other issue, the common good, is not so easy to resolve. Shall we visit friends on our vacation or take a cottage at the beach? The criterion for the decision is "What's best for *us?*" We discuss the pros and cons and come up with a decision we both like. Or we agree to visit the friends this year and plan for the beach trip next summer.

The discussion starts with the premise that we both have good will. We both want to choose what's best for us as a couple. If we can avoid the destructive game of mind reading and second-guessing, we can arrive at a decision. Reaching a decision may require a lot of honest discussion, and the results justify the effort.

Easy to say, hard to carry out, rewarding when done.

We will all be more willing to risk conflict if we accept these basic rules for clean fighting:

> **Stick to the present.**
> **Attack the issue, not the partner.**
> **Hear each other carefully.**
> **Refrain from name-calling.**
> **Refrain from judging motives.**
> **Avoid "you always" and "you never."**
> **Do not compare one another with others.**

Since nobody is perfect, one of us is bound to slip and stray from these ground rules. The first person to recognize what's happening is obliged to point out the slip. When I say to my wife, "You're just like your mother," she will remind me; "Do not compare me with others."

Yes, there will be pain, but it will be constructive pain that strengthens our bond, constructive pain that makes us more willing to listen to each other, pain that is worth seeking and embracing. After each conflict we deal with, there will be a stronger bond between us. Each time we have listened, we have learned something valuable about each other. We can even learn to start a disagreement, trusting from our experience that, in the end, we'll understand and love each other more.

We who pay a surgeon or dentist to hurt us have also learned that the pain of creative and constructive conflict has its own reward.

Marriage means hard work. A good marriage is perhaps the hardest work in the world, and it can be the most rewarding. Marriage is a partnership for growth, the mutual growth of two equal but delightfully different people. And growth means work.

The Third Tool

COURTSHIP

Maybe your eyes met across a crowded room; maybe you met on a blind date. No matter how your courtship started, in the beginning you had nothing invested in each other. But there was something about that first meeting or that first date that was sufficiently rewarding for both of you that you agreed to see each other again.

On the second date, you both put forth a lot of effort. You were good listeners. You were attentive, courteous, respectful. You were fun to be with. And you were both eager for the next date.

Then you had a third date. Perhaps in the first stages of courtship, you liked everything about each other. You were amazed at how much you had in common. However, it was only after your courtship was really underway that you realized that you had differences, that neither of you was perfect, and that you did not always live up to each other's expectations.

Even though your courtship may have had its ups and downs, each of you still agreed that the balance was in favor of continuing to see each other. Your mutual investment was beginning to pay off.

  22

COURTSHIP

What kept this courtship going? Maybe physical attraction was a factor, but there were other ingredients. You set aside time to be together. You made plans. You laughed and played a lot. It was fun. And then there were those romantic sparks.

When I say that a rewarding marriage is a lifelong courtship, I'm not measuring sparks. Sparks may be the kindling that helps get the fire of love started, but who needs kindling when there's a good fire going?

The fire of love can continue burning with the same *controllable* ingredients that got it started: respect, courtesy, attention, best efforts—in other words, continuing courtship.

Some people say that courtship is an unreal time when people are not themselves. George Bernard Shaw wryly observed that when two people are under the influence of the most violent, the most insane, the most delusive, and most transient of passions, the marriage vows require them to swear that they will remain in that excited, abnormal, and exhausting condition until death do them part. I do not agree with Shaw.

I contend that during courtship people are really themselves and that they are their *better* selves. They are good listeners. They are interested in each other's jokes and opinions, experiences, and hurts. They share dreams and feelings. They work hard to make time to be together. It is through this process of repeated time together and repeated mutual rewards that two people come to a mutual decision to marry.

Now I am not so naive as to imagine that all courtships meet the criteria of mutual good things. Some relationships are unhealthy from the beginning—with dependency, or with one person dominating the other. When I say that a good relationship must be a continuing courtship, I'm talking about a healthy relationship that is worth continuing, not one that needs cleaning up; not a relationship of sick dependency: "I couldn't live without you; if you leave me, I'll kill myself"; not a relationship in which one controls the other or requires all of the other's time, energy, and attention. Rather, I'm talking about a relationship between two healthy, relatively independent adults who like themselves—and each other.

Myth

The myth is that a wedding is a marriage and that after the wedding, the whole relationship goes on automatic pilot and needs no further attention. The same two people who had set aside blocks of time just to be together often begin to take each other for granted.

The task is to take each other with gratitude and wonderment, not to take each other for granted. My task is to remind myself that this woman who knows me well still likes me and chooses me above all others. Her task is to remain aware that this man whom she admires most chooses to be with her.

When two people return to the same house at the end of a day's work, rather than an obligation, it *can be* a way of saying, "All things considered, I'd rather be here with you this evening than be anywhere else or with anyone else." That's quite a compliment—a reality renewed daily, one that may never be taken for granted.

To make being together a daily choice is what I am talking about, as well as to continue to celebrate seeing each other, as we did on our third or fourth date.

By contrast, as I drive through the center of town on my way home from work, I observe a husband picking up his wife in the car at the end of their workday. As she gets into the car, they don't look at each other or speak. They don't seem glad to see each other. Maybe they are experiencing the feelings in my Aunt Ruth's adage: "Before you married him, you could eat him up. After you're married, you wish you had."

Choice

The reason we return to the same house at the end of the day is not simply that we're making mortgage payments there. Either of us could choose to go somewhere else. Some people do. We come together, I repeat, by deliberate choice, and this choice is to be celebrated. "I'm glad to see you" is the message we all want to hear, and it is a clear message we are quite capable of giving. "I choose to be with you again tonight, and I will do my part to make our time together honest, respectful, attentive, and fun."

Perhaps 90 percent of all married couples are living well below the level of their relationship potential. That's jargon for "how happy they could be." Their marriages are to some degree dull, routine, unimaginative, boring. The same two people who used to maneuver their schedules in order to make time for courting now go along in a rut. They don't make "dates" or plan special occasions. They may be in the same room in the same house, but that is about all. They seem to think that a marriage license is a license to grow lazy about the relationship that marriage represents.

In our marriage, we call plans for special occasions stepping stones; you know, something to look forward to, something to see us safely on our way. Who plans? Frequently one spouse will take on the role of chief planner. It depends on imagination and temperament. It doesn't matter who suggests a special event as long as both agree to it. As John Wesley said, "A lot of good would be done if nobody cared who got the credit for it."

Another reason why many marriages do not remain exciting is the attitude of ownership: "You belong to me, and I belong to you, and that's that. No further investment. After all, you don't make lifelong payments for what is already rightfully yours, do you?"

Not only do we not own each other, we also keep discovering each other. Every rewarding marriage is a fresh invention; it is unlike any other marriage (although dull ones seem very much alike). What remains the same in all good marriages is the mutual respect and mutual support. What is unique is the way these two individuals make their plans for special times together and carry out their responsibilities. Remember, a wedding is not a marriage; the wedding is the mutual acceptance of a mutual task. This task is not a dreary one; it is the most rewarding work in the world—the work of making two people feel valued, listened to, supported, respected, enjoyed, and loved.

Work for Two

An elderly couple pulled up behind a young couple's car at a traffic light. Seeing the young couple so close to each other, the wife said, "Hiram, when we were young we used to ride close like that in your Model A. Why don't we still ride like that?" Hiram responded, "I ain't moved none!"

Sometimes when a wife in counseling complains, "There is no affection between us," I discover that her perception is that her husband is at fault for not expressing affection. Without input from an observer, she has judged her husband to be the negligent one. When he points out to her that she herself has not been affectionate all week, she realizes their mutual responsibility. "You didn't kiss me" can also be translated "I didn't kiss you." It takes two to kiss or hug.

In no way am I forgetting the importance of commitment. What I am doing is making a distinction between commitment as we would say "committed to an institution or an asylum" and commitment as actively accepting responsibility for a relationship's survival and health.

How about falling out of love? How about, "I love you, but I am no longer 'in love' with you"? Perhaps this statement can be translated, "I am no longer investing energy and time in the relationship. I may be living in the same house with you, sleeping and eating with you, contributing money, but my real treasure—my attention and energy—my real treasure is invested somewhere else." You see, it is true that "where your treasure is, there your heart is also." If I have fallen out of love with you, it is likely that I have long since stopped investing in you. When this happens, it may or may not be too late to try the renewed efforts of courtship, but it may be worth a try.

I am delighted when a young couple in love is willing to raise the question, "Will our love for each other last?" I am not only delighted but encouraged, because they are mature enough to observe marital statistics and to think soberly about their own commitment. I tell them that commitment continues and expresses itself in daily renewal: "I choose you today; I marry you again today." It's like this: If today both of us are respectful, good listeners, attentive, affectionate, supportive, it is more than likely that we will want to be together tomorrow. And if tomorrow we are both respectful and good listeners, honest, attentive, supportive, we'll probably want to be together the next day. It is by daily choice that "'til death do us part" works itself out. The best insurance for the future is today's generous investment in each other. Where your treasure is, there your heart is also.

When a couple continues to court each other day by day, the result is not only "until death do us part," but a love that grows deeper and stronger as the years go on. This continuing courtship is the best insurance and assurance for a joyous and rewarding lifelong commitment. Repeated day by day, it mounts up to "as long as we both shall live."

How do married people continue the courtship? He announces that he has arranged for a babysitter for next Friday night. When they leave the telephone number where the sitter can reach them, it may not be the number for the ritziest restaurant in town, but it is a quiet place where they can have supper and talk—and listen.

How do married couples continue their courtship? She surprises him with the news that next Tuesday will be a special day. It's the anniversary of their first date. And they spend the evening (part of it) talking about their fears and feelings on that first date, as well as their fears and feelings and dreams today.

How do married couples continue their courtship? They agree, even with a lawn that needs mowing and a cluttered kitchen, to go out to a movie they'll both enjoy.

A wedding is the public recognition of a relationship that exists, a relationship now strong enough to risk transplanting from the seedbed of courtship to the field of marriage, which requires a lifetime of daily nurturing through continuing courtship.

The Fourth Tool

LABELS

What we call something determines how we feel about it.

Call it a squirrel and you picture it balanced on its hind legs, twitching a bushy tail, holding an acorn in its front paws. Call the same animal a rodent and observe your own change of feeling. What we call something or someone, how we label things and people and events, makes all the difference. Think of marriage in terms of "settle down," "tied down." Doesn't sound like fun, does it? Then think of marriage as "a chance to grow together."

A label can be a first-rate tool if the label is accurate and if it calls a thing by its right name. On the other hand, the wrong label on a person or on a marriage can do a lot of harm.

As a means of learning to use the tool of labeling, let's examine for accuracy some of the words or phrases we use; for starters, how about rewriting and relabeling "wasting time" or "killing time," at least when we're talking about resting or taking a break. I suppose there's nothing worse to do with time than to kill it. Isn't that murder? Even worse than wasting it.

Now there may be instances when the correct label is wasting or killing

time. Sometimes, though, a more accurate term would be "resting," "taking a breather."

Permission to Play

We tend to come down hard on the people we love when we use inaccurate labels. Husbands and wives can help each other gain personal permission to rest or play just by relabeling. Maybe one of them feels he or she must always keep busy, always be doing something, must never slow up for a minute. The other needs to take a break now and then, to refresh or renew.

How about using the positive term, "permission to play"? How about "respect for the laws of nature," which require work *and* repose, toil *and* play, activity *and* rest, in succession? We have to divide time this way in order to survive.

Permission to pause . . . Industry has learned the value of a coffee break, not so much out of concern for the workers as out of the knowledge that a coffee break results in better productivity. After a pause that refreshes, we work better. Pausing can increase efficiency. Pausers are time users, not time wasters.

Sometimes I meet couples who have lost that freedom to play that was such an important part of their courtship. Either he or she stays so busy that there is not time for being together as friends.

In courting days couples do give themselves permission to play, and this playful togetherness helps build the relationship. Now, in the middle of a demanding life-style, permission to play can help restore that relationship that is more important than all the household duties.

How about "recreation," to re-create one's energies, together with the attitude that it's not only all right but appropriate, praiseworthy, even necessary for the health of a marriage.

Oughts and Shoulds

Perhaps the biggest task of relabeling is in the area of oughts and shoulds. Shoulds and oughts are heavy burdens, and there is not much freedom under their weight.

I remember a young housewife who said, "When I'm cleaning the bathroom, I'm wishing I were outdoors walking the dog. When I'm walking the dog, I tell myself I should be cleaning the bathroom." Her "should" kept her from enjoying a moment of relaxation, a pleasant walk.

Evaluate every "ought," each "should." First, ask "Who said so?" If the pressure comes from someone else or "everybody knows you should," you may have discovered an illusion. If the answer is, "*I* say so, and for this good reason," then it's time to trade in the "should" for an "I will!"

In marriage, oughts and shoulds abound about roles. "The husband should carry out the garbage." "The wife should cook." On and on they go. Who says so? Do these oughts and shoulds come from your parents, society, magazines, TV? Do they reflect the true feelings of you and your spouse?

Relabeling needs to go on as long as we live, since what we call things determines how we feel about them. For example, "I let my wife have friends" implies to some extent that I am in charge of her life. "I recognize and respect her right to have friends" is more accurate. Restating expresses a different attitude and helps to bring about changes in attitude.

When we begin the habit of bringing all of our labels into clear light in order to examine and evaluate each one, we start an endless—but rewarding—task for life. When we become aware of the uniqueness of each beautiful human being (especially the one we married), we give up the stereotypical labels and look in wonder at the real person.

Sayings as Labels

There are labels and sayings that literally immobilize people. My least favorite one is, "Well, I'm the type of person who . . ." When I hear that one, I fear the person is saying, ". . . so don't expect me to learn to act differently; don't expect any progress from me." We label attitudes with sayings. "I can't" is an example. There are occasions, of course, when "I can't" is appropriate: I can't lift the building I'm in. In many instances, though, "I can't" connotes helplessness and impotence when helplessness and impotence are not appropriate. "I can't help feeling this way" leaves no hope. Restate that to read, "I haven't yet learned how to stop worrying when you are late," and the door opens to growth and hope and change. You've heard people say, "I can't help feeling jealous." The truth is they haven't yet learned how to deal with jealousy.

Another good one to tackle is "I've always thought . . ." Find out whether "I have always . . ." subtly implies "and I always will." "Don't ask me to change my stance."

Name-Calling

Name-calling is another disrespectful and dangerous form of labeling. A basic rule of clean fighting is to avoid name-calling. "You're stupid!" is dirty fighting. "I don't see it the way you do" is clean fighting, and it opens the way to dialogue.

This tool of relabeling, which helps us to evaluate everything we say or think about ourselves and others, can constantly help us to correct and refine our perceptions. You see, our unguarded language reveals all too often how we really think.

The wife who asks her husband to "help" her with the dishes is using a dangerous label and an inaccurate one. "Help me" implies that it's really her responsibility and that she is asking, "Won't you be generous by coming to my aid?" Where is it written in stone that washing dishes is gender-specific? It would be more accurate to say, "These dishes we both used need washing; let's do them together."

Perhaps the most hurtful labels in marriage are the trite ones, like: "ball and chain," "my better half," "the old man (lady)." Try "partner" or "equal" and see what possibilities open up with the new label. Exchange "ring in the nose" for "wearing my ring."

In a marriage-counseling session, Frank labeled Cathy as "too emotional." In effect, he was dismissing as unimportant a contribution she could make to their discussion. Feelings are as important as thoughts in dealing with many issues. In fact, when we use feeling and thinking as complementary, as different facets of an issue, we are likely to come up with a better answer for each partner.

One couple I counseled was working very hard on their relationship. Both of them wanted theirs to be a relationship of equals. One day Jim spoke of babysitting their two boys. What did that label imply? Would either of them speak of Martha's time with the children as babysitting? Label it "parenting" for both.

As a couple, resolve: Today we will call each other only respectful names, because what we call each other contributes to how we feel about each other. We will work together to give appropriate labels to everything in our lives: attitudes, actions, events. Calling everything by its right name, its most accurate label, makes all the difference in the world.

The task is to look at every label we use, to study it; is it the right label, the best name for what's happening?

Here are some examples to get you started. It can be fun—and liberating!

In the list that follows, which label fits a given reality best?

manipulating	or	using diplomacy
taking the easy way out	or	taking care of myself
did what I had to do	or	chickened out
lose my temper	or	use my temper
controlling me	or	caring about me
rested	or	killed time
guilt	or	regret
let her (him)	or	respect his (her) right to
lazy	or	low energy level
lost	or	scared
tired	or	lazy
help me	or	work together
clumsy	or	poor coordination
being selfish	or	having self-esteem
fall apart	or	express feelings
fail	or	recognize my limits

Add to the list yourself and enjoy!

The Fifth Tool

REALISM

I once asked a young couple to draw up a list of the qualities they would look for in a spouse if they were choosing a spouse at that moment. I knew their relationship was in trouble when I saw at the top of his list, "She will always be there when I need her."

Relationships sometimes begin with such unrealistic expectations: "I will always be there for you, and you will always be there for me." That's asking more than any two people can possibly deliver.

We cannot ever be perfect mates for each other or always be sufficient for each other's needs. Just as I will not always be generous, loving, and perfect, neither will my spouse.

Do you recall your first love? Maybe it was in college, even in high school. You couldn't see enough of each other. Both of you thought that if only you two could be together, at least twenty-seven hours a day, "just you and me, baby," life would be a dream. Each of you was all the other needed to make life perfect. If you recall this, then you also recall what happened next. One of you got tired of the constant togetherness, maybe both of you did, but one had the courage to back off. When one of you realized that being together like Siamese twins was not the route to the stars, that was when you began to discover that there *is* no perfect other; there *is* no perfect relationship. Unless one of you learned nothing from the experience and went off to look for another perfect mate, you accepted this reality.

When Henry and Rachel began dating each other, they saw each other as the perfect choice, Mr. and Ms. Right. They were amazed at how much they had in common—the same interests, the same tastes. By the time they came for counseling two years later, both were disillusioned. Henry liked camping in the woods or at the beach. Rachel's idea of the outdoor life was lounging on a balcony off their room at the Holiday Inn or tanning beside the pool.

Looking for the mirror image of self as the perfect mate is looking for an illusion. There is no such person on earth. To require perfection is to ensure failure, whether the perfection is sought in oneself or in the other.

Accept the Imperfect

What is left, then, if—no, *since*—there is no perfect mate for every individual on earth? The first task is to recognize and admit imperfection in self and in the other. Just as I cannot be all things to you, you cannot be all things to me. This admission is the positive pain of reality.

The second task is to forgive each other for not living up to unrealistic expectations or, perhaps, to forgive ourselves for having such unrealistic expectations in the first place.

The third task is to see each other's imperfections in the perspective of the whole person. True, his table manners are not the best, but what a generous, supportive, fun person he is. True, she sometimes fails to be ready on time, but what a sensitive, loving person she is.

Perspective

When my wife taught public speaking, she would hold up a large white poster board before the class. In the middle of the 20″ × 30″ sheet was a black dot about the size of a dime. "What do you see?" she would ask. Inevitably the answer came: "A black dot!" "But what else do you see?" Then she would point out that the black dot was a very small percentage of the whole surface of the white poster. That's the task—to see the whole person, not just the flaws.

There is no person on earth who can suit me to a T, and neither can I suit anyone else in all ways. I have many good qualities, but I am not perfect. We are not perfect, but we complement one another. We work at listening to each other. We hear and we care. Our job is not to heal the other, to fix the other, or to remake the other in our own image and likeness.

Finally, the task is for each of us to nurture ourselves, to believe we are able to take care of ourselves, to trust ourselves. At times, each of us will be alone and lonely. At times, I will need to be alone with my thoughts, with my hurt or high feelings. I will value my specific, special, and unique self. I will let my feelings flow. I will need to ask the God of my authentic self, of my good judgment, of my intuition and my dreams to show me my path. Although I will never be the perfect mate (or find one), I will keep on growing.

But no one can develop such self-concepts as "accepted," "valued," or "worthwhile" all alone. We have to have the affirming mirror of others.

However, we are slow learners, or partial learners. One part of us knows the truth of imperfection; another part of us is still so determined to have the perfect relationship that sometimes we are untrue to ourselves. We try to say what someone else wants to hear, to do what someone else wants us to do. We pretend that there can be a perfect relationship. And the more another person responds to our facade, our pretense, the unhappier we become. The error we make is in telling ourselves, "I don't care what it takes, I am going to make this relationship work and last forever." If we do this, eventually we will begin to feel cramped and confined as we try to live up to another's expectations. We think we must be everything our partner desires. We don't dare to assert our independence, because independence may be interpreted as a loss of love.

The antidote to this dilemma is to believe that "I am lovable as I am, warts and all." If another were to respond to our fictitious person, there would be no true meeting. However, if another can find us lovable as we are, a healthy relationship is possible.

Besides, there are other friends or hobbies to provide some of the things each of us needs. Our marriage may have begun with the expectation that couples can be everything to each other, but that expectation will eventually prove to be a myth.

Ann was determined to have a perfect marriage. Bill meant everything to her. She would always agree, she would like what he liked, learn to love each one of his friends, enjoy whatever he enjoyed. She would like every one of his relatives and become his mother's daughter. She would celebrate holidays exactly the way Bill's family had always done. When Ann came to realize that she was exhausted and depressed, she wondered why. She was angry with herself. "Will the real Ann please stand up?" After counseling, Ann learned that when she gets angry, she can usually trace it back to not speaking up soon enough, to not asserting her individuality. Never, for the sake of so-called peace and harmony, should we deny our own experiences and convictions.

When Bill and Ann came for marriage counseling, I had the image of a frustrated woman and a bewildered man. Hadn't she always said yes? Not being a mind reader, Bill supposed that her going along was authentic. For her part, Ann felt empty, a nothing. Had she married the wrong person? Had Bill married a clone of himself? He was tired of making all the decisions. She was tired of being the "perfect wife."

It took us some time to bring to light the expectations they had accepted, such as: A wife should always please her husband, always agree, always like what he likes. No wonder Ann was exhausted and empty and angry with herself. No wonder she bewildered Bill.

Clone or Self

What Ann and Bill learned about themselves was that they held some unrealistic expectations, some shoulds and oughts that neither could live up to. From their growing pains during counseling, Ann learned that Bill didn't expect her to be his shadow or his clone. Of course it was all right for her to have opinions and tastes and friends and interests of her own, either like his or different from his. She didn't have to be the perfect wife, whatever that might be. She became a better wife by being herself. It wasn't easy. Ann was scared at first to want something Bill didn't want, and she had spoiled him to the point that he had to work through their mutual identity crisis. When Bill suggested inviting John and Lynne over for dinner and Ann said she didn't want to, he did a double take. Ann explained that what she preferred was a quiet evening for the two of them; that wasn't hard for Bill to take.

Gradually, they developed more honesty between them. They came to like the new person they discovered in the other and in themselves.

When we put our spouse on a pedestal and declare our mate perfect, we live under an illusion. It is also hard to be close to someone who's standing on a pedestal above you.

We are geniuses at setting up two unacceptable extremes: Either I'm perfect or I'm no good. The truth is that there is a comfortable point on the continuum between total perfection at one extreme and total evil at the other. We can find a comfortable point we can live with, like "pretty good" or "most of the time."

To have to be in control all the time is to have no control. It leaves us no freedom of choice. Some things require our best efforts, but not all things. Some things don't always deserve our best—like vacuuming the apartment. A seasonal, thorough cleaning, yes; but this time "a lick and a promise" might be perfectly acceptable.

If we begin with the premise "Anything worth doing is worth doing, whether well or poorly," then we are free to pick and choose in a hierarchy those things that really *do* deserve our best efforts, or at least our better efforts. Talking to each other deserves our best attention, but a casual chat with a neighbor in passing requires a little less effort.

Let's face it: We have both married a person with flaws, a lovable person who has some flaws. And can we add, "And that's okay!"?

The Sixth Tool

TRUST

Trusting another person is always somewhat of a risk. When we're dealing with someone we love, isn't the risk of trusting preferable to the alternative?

Trust can happen in two ways: It can be earned, or it can be donated to another, given freely without being earned. Let me explain.

The first is obvious—and easier: I learn to trust you because you have always or usually been trustworthy and truthful in our relationship. You have given me no reason to doubt your word, your fidelity, your love. And you have given me many reasons to believe you, to trust you.

On the other hand, donating trust when it has not been earned is courageous, more risky. It is a decision I reach in spite of your past dishonesty. I have forgiven you, and in deciding to trust you again today, I give up suspicion and I give up playing detective.

The good results?

As I trust you, I place a wholesome pressure on you to live up to my trustful expectations.

Isn't it true that people tend to live up to—or down to—expectations?

That is, if I trust you even when you're lying, you are likely to feel some motivation to "clean up your act."

This Special Person

Now I'm certainly not saying that trust alone can make another person honest or trustworthy, but we're not talking about just any person. We're not talking about people who will play another for a sucker or take advantage. We're talking about you and me, about average, weak, good-willed people who want to grow and respond to each other in a good relationship.

So, in the light of my trusting you, you're likely to be or to become more worthy of my trust. And believe me, if you'll just give me another chance, I'll show you I can be trusted!

On the other hand, if you and I were always suspecting each other and accusing and checking up on one another, eventually one of us is likely to say, "I may as well be guilty as charged; if I'm going to be condemned anyway, I may as well be guilty."

Some people say that only fools trust, that only fools believe and accept all things. They point out the danger that some other person will take advantage of the one who trusts. Again, we're not talking about trusting everybody; we're talking about trust in a marriage. We're talking about a special relationship—and the trust that is fundamental for its growth.

Mutual trust is the goal. The one who begins to trust, the one who initiates trust, is the winner. And it is contagious.

Tyler and Alice had been married for almost two years. Toward the end of their first year, Tyler had an affair with a fellow graduate student. It was short-lived, lasting about three months. Tyler was contrite, remorseful. He regretted the affair and learned from it how important his marriage was to him. What he wanted most of all was a good marriage with Alice.

However, Alice was still uneasy. For the past nine months Tyler had been the model husband—faithful, sensitive, honest, and affectionate; just about all she could ask for. But the memory of the affair nagged and tormented her. Her pain was her distrust. His pain was not being trusted.

Forgive and Remember

When I meet with couples in pain like Tyler and Alice, I wish I could talk to the person who invented the term "forgive and forget." "Forgive and forget" is an unfortunate piece of advice because it is unattainable. We can never forget events that were either poignantly painful or intensely delightful. We may not be able to remember mundane events, like what we ate for breakfast on October 26, 1986, but we will never forget our first broken heart or our first date with our spouse.

Alice's task is to remember Tyler's affair in the light of the present. "Today he is faithful to me; today he loves me. He is a good husband who has learned from his mistakes." The task for all of us is to do two things with past mistakes: We forgive them, and we learn from them, even while we cannot forget them.

Having learned from our mistakes and having forgiven them, we can spend our energy on the present. Today is all we have. Alice could destroy their marriage by dwelling on the past, by making Tyler "pay" for the rest of his life for a regrettable event from the past. She could question Tyler every time he is a few minutes late; she could sniff around his head when she embraces him; she could examine his handkerchiefs and billfold; she could live in constant suspicion. She could dwell on the past.

Or, she could choose to live in the present. Today, she has a faithful husband. Today they are both working on their relationship. That's precisely why they have come for counseling.

In counseling they forgive themselves and each other for having been less than perfect. They accept each other's forgiveness. Tyler, for his part, will learn to distinguish between guilt and regret. Guilt he no longer has; he is forgiven. Regret he can live with. Now they can both dwell on the present, in the present.

In the present we find many opportunities to trust. We interpret motives in a positive way. We respect each other's right to privacy. We do not snoop or play detective, or hire one.

Areas of privacy related to trust include wallet and purse, mail, notes, and calendars. In our marriage we extend this trust of privacy to telephone calls. When one of us has answered the telephone, the other does not ask, "Who was that?" We respect privacy. If I want to tell my wife who called, fine. Usually, though, she's reading the evening paper and doesn't care to hear that the firemen's auxiliary called for a donation. And, if I didn't respect her right to privacy, how could she plan for my surprise birthday party?

Trust also means standing close to each other in the face of all others. In visits with Ed's family, Nell felt isolated. As she saw it, when she and Ed arrived at his parents' home, he would drop her off to stay with the women while he went off with the men. When Nell confronted Ed with her view, he was surprised. In his family, the men and the women had always accepted this arrangement. "I feel abandoned," she said. "I don't expect you to hold my hand throughout the visit, but I do want you to stand by me. I want to know that you care about me when we're with your family as truly as when we're in our own home, maybe more so."

When Ed began paying attention to Nell at his family's gatherings, both Ed and Nell were delighted at the response from some of the others. Other in-laws didn't like the traditional separation-by-gender either, but nobody else had had the courage to take the step. Nobody else thought things could be any different from the way they had always been. When Ed and Nell were clearly a pair, others followed suit. The family visits took on a new life, as husbands and wives talked to other husbands and wives.

It's a comfort to know you can trust the fact that your spouse will be there for you in the presence of others, that, for instance, at parties you will find a comfortable—and trusting—stance somewhere between these two unacceptable extremes: the spouses who part company the moment they arrive and never see each other again until leaving time, or the spouses who cling to each other all evening and who might as well have stayed at home for all the mingling they do. Trusting couples make occasional contact with each other throughout the party—a loving glance across the room, a touch on the shoulder in passing, a wink. They are conscious of each other's presence, trusting each other's ability to enjoy the party, trusting that neither needs a warden or a guardian.

I think I will never forget my wife's beautiful trust as she prepared for her first business trip out of town after our wedding. As she was packing, she said she'd miss me. She also said, "Why don't you invite Betty (our friend) out for supper while I'm gone?"

Another moment that isn't so beautiful stands out in my memory. Several weeks after I had stopped drinking, I was feeling good, even a little giddy in my new freedom. My wife looked over at me where I sat in my favorite rocking chair, and she said with concern, "Honey, have you had a drink?"

Of course I was offended. Didn't she trust me? We had a frank talk then and there. We agreed that trust implies interpreting events in their best possible light. This is a lesson we can use often: Safely presume the best.

Trust also entails hearing each other's questions as they are spoken, without looking for ulterior motives or hidden agenda. Accept questions at face value.

Everyday we will say to each other anew: Trust me, and I'll be worthy of your trust. And I'll trust you, because it's the only way we have to freedom, to growth, to respect; to deeper trust.

The Seventh Tool

FRIENDSHIP

By the time couples come to marriage counseling, they are often acting like enemies and thinking of each other as the enemy.

The seventh tool, friendship, comes to the rescue. This tool says to wife and husband, "How would two friends deal with this issue?" When I pose this question to an angry couple, you can almost feel the heaviness lifting. They are sometimes not aware that they are treating one another like enemies or antagonists or competitors.

These two people were friends when they first came together. They felt safe with each other. They probably were friends before they were lovers.

And certainly they didn't decide to marry in order to destroy each other. They did not enter marriage for the avowed purpose of making life mutually miserable. They came together to be friends and lovers, to be good for each other.

What is included in our idea of "friend"?—one who accepts me as I am, one who listens to me, one who will not laugh at me, one who answers honestly, one who avoids sarcasm, one who sees me as an equal. A friend apologizes when he or she has been wrong.

A friend is someone I can laugh with—we don't take ourselves too seriously. If there's security in having a friend, it's the freedom to cry, to be less than perfect, to be human, to disagree safely.

A friend is freely chosen, out of desire, not need. "I want you" is healthy. "I need you" can be a sick dependency. The wholesome message is "I can get along without you, but my life will be richer with you in it."

A friend gives us the benefit of the doubt. Couples need to develop simple signals to help each other restore the atmosphere of friendship, on the spot. It can be the peace symbol or a tug at the ear or upraised arms (as in surrender)—whatever we agree to recognize as a reminder. Then we can laugh at ourselves for acting like enemies and resume confronting the issue as the friends we really are.

When we couples stop acting like friends, we begin to interpret each other's responses negatively. A question becomes an accusation. "Did you bring in the newspaper?" is interpreted as "You should have." What I suggest is to interpret each other's questions and statements in the best possible light rather than negatively. The truth is that by interpreting positively one is more likely to interpret correctly, because we are friends, not enemies. See a question as a clean question. "Did you bring in the newspaper?" is asked simply to save a trip to the front porch, not for the sake of criticizing. Further, help each other become accustomed to clean questions, without any hidden agenda; preface a question with "This is a clean question, not an accusation."

Test of Friendship

One's complaint may be "You're spending too much time on your job; you're depriving me of your company. You're running away from me. You don't like being with me."

And how *would* friends deal with this complaint? First, a friend would trust the good will of the other. "Surely you *do* like me; it must be that you are unaware of how much I want your company. Or maybe I'm not much fun to be with these days. How can I help? How can I make being with me more rewarding?" I will tell you, "I want more time with you."

However, even the best of friends cannot always be available. As in all friendships, there are times when one partner is unavailable, physically or emotionally, for a time. The one who is left alone will take responsibility for filling his or her time instead of wallowing in self-pitying loneliness.

"One thing I have learned since I've been married to David," said Mary, "is that I can't *make* him talk to me. I can't say to him, 'Tell me what's bothering you.' I have to find a way to give the message that I'm here for him—if and when he's ready for me." She has learned to communicate silently or in patient words that she is willing to listen.

Trying to force a partner to reveal his or her innermost thoughts is a violation of privacy. It is not respectful. It is not the attitude of a true friend.

Friendship in marriage includes the reality that we cannot be all things to each other all the time. However, these two people know each other well; they know how to heal each other; and, brother, do they know how to hurt each other! Each of them knows where the other's hot button is, and each one knows how to press it. Apply friendship to this fact, and we know what to do: Handle with care; heal; don't hurt. A friend would never deliberately hurt a friend.

Open, Sesame

Do you agree with me that every one of us wants to talk, wants to share dreams and fears and hopes with someone? That someone is a person who can be trusted. Each one of us can say, "I want to talk, and I *will* talk—when it is safe to talk, when my words will be heard, not rebutted; when my sharing is accepted, not ridiculed." When either spouse complains that the other will not talk, this is the question for the complainer: How can I make it safe for you to talk to me?

No Pedestal

Friendship tells us something else about a relationship: "On a pedestal" is no place to be, for him or for her. On a pedestal is the opposite of equality, and it is only between equals that we can have a healthy relationship.

And how about carrying equality all the way to the point of saying that true intimacy requires equal authority? Neither partner is the boss; neither rules the other. As in all true partnerships, the leadership can shift from situation to situation, depending on a partner's competence, energy, health, or other factors of the moment. For example, in our marriage, my wife defers to me in matters of decorating. She says, "Cranor can envision how something will look, and I trust his judgment." We still confer, and Rita still has a veto, but I am the acknowledged leader in decor, just as she is the acknowledged leader in matters of organization and logical planning. As friends, we are definitely not in competition with each other.

Listen carefully for words that are contradictory to friendship: "win" or "lose," "get one up on you," "owe you one," "gotcha." Terms like these are signals to remind us we're not acting like friends. A good test of how you're doing is: If you can substitute "I'm out to get you" for a statement, then you are not talking like friends.

Being friends in marriage is more important today then ever before. Back in the days when marriage was a mutual dependency of function (to lapse into sociological jargon), when he was the breadwinner and physical protector and she was the homemaker and caretaker, friendship was less of an issue. Today, though, many spouses are financially independent; we look at the interpersonal and subjective inner dimension; we look to each other for support of a different kind, for comfort, for companionship, for healing—from the hurts of the competitive and cruel world.

Equals

Keep coming back to the point of equality, because friendship presumes equality. Equality is essential to a healthy marriage between two thinking and feeling and trusting adults.

I would go so far as to say that equality is the gauge of a healthy relationship. And it has so many facets. Does either of us feel insecure, threatened, in any way afraid in the relationship? Does either of us feel dominated? Here, we're not looking for a villain, because the unhealthy game of domination-submission requires two players. In order to be dominated, the second player has to submit.

Marriage is the union of two people who are self-supporting and support-ive to each other; of two relatively independent people who have chosen to share a large part—not all—of their lives with each other; of two people who are happily obligated by choice, not by shoulds and oughts. In other words, it is the union of two friends who rejoice in each other, who have respect and joy in each other's lives.

The Eighth Tool
DISTINCTIONS

The eighth tool involves making distinctions. Keep careful distinctions among three aspects of a relationship—friendship, affection, and sex. Distinguish not for the sake of separating the three but for the sake of respecting each aspect for its own worth. Friendship, affection, and sex are like the three legs of a tripod on which a relationship stands solid.

Friendship

We have identified friendship as the seventh tool for maintaining the relationship, for repairing it. List again for yourself the qualities of a friend:

one you can trust,
one you are at ease with,
one who takes you as you are,
one with whom you can be yourself,

one who enjoys your company,
one who likes you,
one who is supportive,
one who is not judgmental,
one you want to share things with—joy, a joke, trouble,
    pain, a dream . . .

These qualities, and others, we usually identify with our marriage partner. That is, if we are each other's friend. We can be friends to each other twenty-four hours a day. We can be affectionate many times in a day when we both want to express affection, and we can be sexual partners when we both want to be.

Affection

No two people have the same appetite for either affection or sex. One is more open to touching than the other; one has a stronger sex drive than the other. The reason for distinguishing clearly between sex and affection is simple: It is necessary to assure that both affection and sex are authentic and mutual.

Couples who fail to keep this distinction clear end up having less affection and less sex. If the distinction is not made, then the partner with the weaker sex appetite may tend to shy away from affection, interpreting affection as an overture for sex. If he or she interprets affection as a request for sex, then that partner will not feel as free to respond spontaneously to affection. Without this distinction between affection and sex, the need to touch and to be touched gets confused with the desire to have sex, when all one really wants at the moment is a little body contact of the mildest sort. Sex is not the only way to celebrate our love.

In order to keep the distinction between affection and sex clear, here is a practical contract to which each partner agrees: "When either of us expresses affection in any way—a kiss, a touch, a hug, a pat on the fanny, the other agrees to accept that expression of affection in itself, for its own sake, at face value, without any further intimation." To say it another way, "When I hug you, it's because I like to hug you. Period." The agreement continues, "When I want to have sex, I'll make it clear; there'll be no doubt about what I'm asking. And you, of course, are free to say yes or no."

It's important to keep freedom and spontaneity in a relationship. Notice how often people in love touch each other—and how respectfully. Physical touch, as long as it is respectful and authentic, supports life. One can die without it.

Touch keeps us alive in more ways than one. During World War II infants were whisked by train out of London to country estates used as nurseries. There were many babies, few attendants. The death rate among the infants was high. Reason? Not enough holding, cuddling, nurturing. From the moment of birth, an infant needs to be held, talked to, sung to—needs to feel the warmth of another's skin. Without this affectionate attention, an infant can die or at least suffer emotional damage. At the other end of one's life, in old age, people need the comfort of touch. A wise nurse says to family members around a deathbed: "Don't just sit there; stand by the bed, touch your loved one from time to time, hold your loved one's hand; it's very comforting."

From birth to death human beings need touch. To touch another is like a grounding with the universe; it is to be in touch with all of life. Consider the opposite of touch: untouchable, which equals devaluing or even rejection.

Touch gives reassurance, and reassurance that we are lovable is something we all need often. We can even speak of the magic of touch as a life-giver. See Michelangelo's fresco of creation: God touching the outstretched lifeless hand of Adam, to give life!

Lucky are those children whose parents express affection for each other in their presence.

Sex

And then there's sex. Sex is a unique way to say "I love you" that can be replaced by nothing else. Sex is a language of eloquence without words.

Words, however, the right words, can help immensely to keep sex in marriage meaningful, exciting, comforting, fun. The words serve as directions and encouragement as we guide one another in the discovery of our wonderful bodies. No matter how much experience one has had with no matter how many partners, genuine lovemaking with one's spouse at any single moment is a unique experience.

Give positive feedback and directions, not criticism. Since everyone's chief sex organ is the brain, a very sensitive organ, spouses have to be careful not to deflate each other's ego. Whenever one spouse accuses the other of being a lousy lover, I suggest that the accusation is a witness against the accuser. Each of us must take responsibility for our own body: Each of us must tell our partner what we want, what is pleasurable. The lover, who is not a mind reader, needs direction—for *this* event. Making love today is not the same as the last time. We are not in the same place, and we need to give each other indications of what pleases *now*.

Getting a back massage is a good model for sexual communication. What makes for a good back rub is good directions: "higher, easy does it, right there," etc. The goal is that we become as comfortable talking about sex as we are when receiving a back rub. Or, as comfortable talking about sex as we are talking about food. We have no trouble pointing out how we like our coffee or our eggs or what toppings we want on our pizza. Why do we play guessing games with sex?

The degree of comfort we're looking for requires a lot of work. We begin by calling the parts of our bodies by their rightful names and by being comfortable with each other's nude body. Just as we do not call a nose a smelly-poo, neither do we call a vagina or a penis anything else—some self-conscious circumlocution. We work to overcome generations of attitudes about not talking about sex.

Each His Own

In marriage we do not own each other's body. We do not own each other, body or soul. In marriage each of us remains a person in charge; sharing, yes, but basically responsible for herself, himself.

Do we think we own each other? A good test is to ask the question: When one spouse suggests making love, is the other free to say yes or no? The goal: Either of us is free to initiate making love. Each of us is free to say yes or no. When there's a yes, we know it's mutual and sincere—out of desire, not duty.

Some people have the idea that being married means having sex available at any time, on demand. Such is not the case. As attractive as sex whenever wanted may sound (get an inflatable doll?), it's not nearly as rewarding as a genuine and enthusiastic positive response. We would rather experience genuine lovemaking three times a week than halfhearted intercourse six times a week!

We all need to be reassured that we are lovable, desirable, desired: just the opposite of taking each other for granted. We learn to give this message over and over again: I find you attractive. We learn to communicate our own feelings before we can expect our partner to respond.

The reason for keeping a careful distinction among these aspects of a relationship—friendship, affection, and sex—is not at all to separate them but, rather, to preserve respect for each of them and to relish each of them in turn.

Couples I have counseled report with enthusiasm what freedom they have experienced by keeping these distinctions and by making the contract to accept any expression of affection for its own sake. The early stages of courtship included lots of affection, and it was great. It still is.

We are friends to each other at every moment.

We are affectionate with each other at frequent moments.

We make love at special moments.

The Ninth Tool

RESPECT

"**I** never laid a hand on her," Todd said in defense. "All I did was to hold her down on the bed when she wouldn't talk to me!"

"Todd," I said, "do you like to be held against your will?"

The first use of this tool is respect for each other's character, each other's body. I ask every couple to make the contract that Todd and Elizabeth made: "As long as we are together, I will touch you only with respect and affection." When physical violence in any form creeps in—be it holding or blocking or slapping or hitting—respect goes fast. The one doing it loses respect for self and for the one who tolerates the violence. The one permitting the violence loses respect for self and for the violent one.

It is never enough to say, "He (she) drove me to it." We can always turn and walk away until we recapture our cool. There is never an adequate excuse for violence. Violence indicates a high level of frustration. Violence tells us that respect has left the relationship and must be brought back into it.

Many couples split at that very moment when they could enter an exciting phase of their marriage. They speak of irreconcilable differences because two stubborn heads have butted. It could have become very reconcil-able respect if both had listened to each other.

"It hurts when you're not heard." As the young couple sat in my office, neither one listening to the other, he was thinking only of himself and his own wounds, not yet stretching to imagine how not being heard felt to her.

Look Again

Respect means literally to take a second look, which implies that there has been a first look. And there has been. There was surely a time when both spouses felt respected, appreciated. Then gradually there came a day when, as one wife put it, "We neglected to notice each other except as partners in a project."

Look At Me

What we require of our children is a good custom to adopt between us: Look at me when I talk to you. Or, better still, "I will look at you when I talk to you, and I hope you will do the same."

Here are two unique human beings, a unique couple, equal in dignity. Both have the right to be treated with respect.

When spouses in counseling are reporting a conversation they had between sessions, I find myself trying to supply the tone of voice the reporting party actually used. So often the tone of voice in what is being recalled makes a lot of difference. Sometimes I ask couples to tape-record some of their conversations. People are frequently not aware exactly how they sound to each other.

Climate of Respect

We're familiar these days with the concept of unconditional acceptance: I love you as you are. I accept you even though I don't like everything about you. This is the climate we want, a comfortable climate in which we can all do our best growing. We're accepting, not monitoring; we're being accepted, not monitored.

The reality is that unconditional love does not change another person but provides the proper *climate* for change. Change is the business of the person being loved—at his pace, in her own way.

In rehabilitating society's offenders, as in marriage, there is a clear distinction between reforming someone (impossible) and creating a safe climate in which that person can grow. Because of love, Beauty's Beast is freed to become his best self.

Each of us is aware that she is rooting for *him*, and he is on *her* side.

This acceptance is quite different from entering marriage with the idea of changing one's spouse, an idea that does not work. Reform of another person is not a purpose of marriage.

Remake

Let's admit, though, that there is in each one of us a tendency to want to change someone else. I used to say to my wife, "Honey, a simple yes or no will do"—in answer to a question. She was wise enough and self-assured enough to say, "A simple yes or no may do for you; you answer in your way, and I'll answer in my way." That spells respect.

There is the temptation to remake the other in our own image and likeness. Even if remaking a spouse were permissible or possible, it still wouldn't work. We would soon reject the person who permitted such manipulation—if that person didn't reject us first! What attracted us in the beginning was the uniqueness of the other person. This uniqueness is to be respected, not changed. Who would find his or her own clone an exciting partner?

It is not being different from one another that separates us; it is the lack of respect for those differences. Our chief difference is our main attraction: You are female, I am male. This gender difference attracted us to each other because we respected the fact that one is man, the other is woman.

It is the atmosphere of acceptance that makes changing myself a thing I can risk. If I feel that my wife accepts me as I am, warts and all, then I am comfortable enough to do some growing. On the other hand, if I think she is watching me critically, then I will be too uncomfortable to risk trying something new. And as for her, she really wants to grow and change as truly as I do; what she needs is someone to accept her as she is so that she can safely risk moving out of old habits and develop new ways of coping and responding.

If we think of change as developing one's potential, as growing, then we can talk about helping each other change.

Respect requires the admission, once and for all, that we are equal and alike in only two ways: our equal dignity and our right to be treated with respect. In all other ways, we are different. The list is endless; here is a partial one, to be considered item by item:

FOOD: quantity, variety, setting, its meaning to a person; eat in or out, formally or informally; snacking between meals, eating in bed; table manners.

SLEEP:	night person, morning person; amount of sleep; naps, short or long; tolerance of noise, light, sunlight; window closed, open, or cracked; how many blankets.
SEX:	frequency, meaning, variety, ardor; how romantic or routine.
ORDER AND CLEANLINESS:	personal hygiene, from teeth to toes; tolerance for clutter, dirt, dishes.
PRIVACY:	bathroom, mail, telephone, wallet and handbag, friendships, confidences.
TIME ALONE:	no two people have the same need; all need some time alone.
TOGETHERNESS:	how much, how often, what kind.
HOBBIES:	same and/or different; social situations; other friends, large parties or intimate gatherings.

No two couples are alike. Some are quite satisfied with little sharing of time and space:

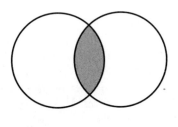

○○   63   ○○

Others need more:

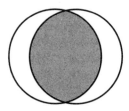

What is intolerable, killing, smothering, contradictory to growth is when a couple tries to act like Siamese twins:

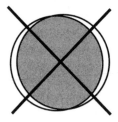

—when a trip to the bathroom is the only acceptable separateness.

When a relationship begins, one may want to touch before the other is ready. This is the first clue to "differences to be respected." It is rare that any two people are at "the same place" at the same time. One will respectfully wait for the other, compromise for the other. When my wife is out of town, I never make the bed. When my wife is in town, we—one of us or both of us together—make the bed every morning. Making the bed is important to her, and I respect this needless eccentricity. Just joking.

Communication

Respect for differences applies especially to communication. No two people speak exactly the same language. We may not presume that we have understood the message just because we have heard the words spoken. Rather, check it out: "I understood you to say . . ." It takes very little time, and it makes communication possible.

Here's an example: "Is your friend coming Saturday or Sunday?" That's a clean question, as it stands. If the person hearing the question takes it at face value, then the communication is achieved. However, wouldn't some of us, at least some of the time, read between the lines and reply, "Don't you want him to come?"

Since we are likely to interpret messages negatively when they concern us, it is a respectful habit between spouses to concentrate on a positive interpretation. "That's a new tie, isn't it?" "You don't like it?" What *would* be an appropriate response to "That's a new tie, isn't it?" How about, "Yes, it is."

When efforts at communication reach an impasse, respect suggests taking each other's side. That is, tell each other what you hear the other saying and feeling until each can say, "Yes, that's exactly what I mean." It may take several attempts to express the other's point of view without rebuttal, without sarcasm or editorializing. It's hard to complete that communication loop sometimes; it's worth the effort. The exercise of putting myself in your place, of hearing myself state your position can create a lot of insight for me. And for you, it's a good feeling, knowing that you have been heard.

Respect has many ramifications: freedom to be one's self, freedom to be different; freedom to be quiet, to experiment, to risk, to err; freedom to rest.

We are not responsible for each other's conduct. Neither of us wants to disgrace the family; both of us want the best for our family. We cannot control each other's choice of friends or hobbies. We can suggest; we can advise. We can respect each other's right to make decisions. When you can't change the facts, try bending your attitude. Call it respect for reality.

Respect spells space: enough space to satisfy the needs of each person for intimacy and distance; to feel both connected and separate; to learn to live with the sign NO TRESPASSING. It is difficult to move from deep connectedness to solid separateness and back again. It's a dance more difficult than any on the ballroom floor.

Timing

One difference to be respected is each person's response to a disagreement. One will find it hard to tolerate any misunderstanding and will be eager, even anxious, to get things settled right away. The other may need a cooling-off period, a brief or not so brief time to lick wounds. A couple I remember well had trouble making this respectful adjustment. It was Tom who couldn't bear for any unpleasantness to remain unsettled, even for a brief time. Denise, on the other hand, was seldom willing to thrash things out on the spot. As she put it, she needed to sit in her corner and think about it all for a spell, then talk about it. When Tom would urge talking it out then and there, she felt pressured—and she rebelled. What they finally discovered was this difference in timing. He learned to wait a few minutes. She learned to shorten the time she made Tom wait.

Two other issues closely involved in respect are privacy and protectiveness: privacy—to strive for it; protectiveness—to avoid it.

The right to some privacy is a basic human need. I contend that a child deserves at least one drawer he can call his own. We do not open his drawer without his permission, not because he has shameful secrets in there but because he has a right to privacy, to a space he can call his own.

As for opening mail addressed to another person, apart from being a federal offense, it is a no-no.

It is also a good idea for each partner to have a personal space for privacy: a quiet corner, a special chair, even a room for one's own use. And that space—her desk, his workbench, her weight room, his sewing room—can be kept according to the standards of the individual.

Living as a couple certainly does not imply being responsible for each other's conduct. Examine this remark: "When you monopolized the conversation at the party, you embarrassed me." How is the wife's or husband's conduct a reflection on the spouse? Are we each other's keeper? I think not. We deserve to liberate ourselves from running two lives. Being responsible for one's own conduct is a full-time job. Running two lives is too much to require of any person. Because we care, we can suggest that "at last night's party you monopolized the conversation." See the difference?

And a protector is something no responsible adult needs. Did you ever notice how some spouses come to the rescue when someone asks the partner a heavy question? Work on respecting your spouse's ability to answer for himself, to look after herself.

We began this chapter talking about providing a safe place for each other. Isn't that exactly what we all want, an environment where it's safe for me to be myself; to be trusted, to be respected? That which we all want we can provide for the other.

There is no tradition that teaches us to live with each other as equals in mutual respect and trust. In this we are pioneers.

The Tenth Tool

SHARING

The tenth tool, sharing, might be the hardest to use because it requires the skill of striking a careful balance between independence on the one hand and engulfment on the other. To put it positively, sharing means a healthy interdependence: a sharing of responsibilities, a sharing of things and dollars, a sharing of space and time.

First of all, there is the shared responsibility for the marriage's health, maintenance, and repair. When two people marry, they agree to share much of their lives, with less concern for fifty-fifty than for mutual needs and abilities. Both partners contribute according to their abilities; both receive according to their needs, in sickness and in health.

What must be shared? Decisions, parenting, long- and short-range planning, income, budget, bills, purchases, savings, home, yard, decorating, meal-planning, grocery shopping, cooking, cleaning, laundry, cars, entertaining, relationships with relatives and neighbors, and dreams. The list is long.

Looking at this long list, the goal for a couple becomes: How can we share between us what must be done in ways that are acceptable to both of us?

Messages like the following are sure signs that the tool of sharing needs to be used: "He doesn't want a wife; he wants a maid and a mistress." "She doesn't want a husband; she wants a handyman and a checkbook." When somebody feels used or put upon, it's a sure sign that sharing needs to come into the picture.

Job for Each

What we do share, most of all, is responsibility for the relationship.

Responsibility for the relationship means that no one person is responsible for being available, for settling disputes, for making decisions, for planning social engagements, for making dates with each other, for arranging holiday celebrations and outings, for thinking about the future with imagination.

Just when a couple returns from the honeymoon with the best of intentions to have the best marriage possible, heavy responsibility awaits them. They have come together from two different families. Each one has brought an inheritance. Let's picture the inheritance as two large boxes in the middle of the living room when they cross the threshold. Inside these boxes, one from his family and one from her family, are not china and silver and crystal—nothing material. These inherited boxes contain shoulds and oughts, expectations, attitudes, roles, beliefs, and values; in other words, clear—but possibly different—pictures of what a wife is like and what a husband is like. These boxes are to be opened with respect and examined with care.

Together, in the months and years ahead, this new husband and wife will share the responsibility of deciding what to keep among these heirlooms, what to discard, and what to modify to fit their unique needs.

The contents of these boxes cover a range, from how decisions are made in a family, through all aspects of parenting, all the way to such details as when to open Christmas presents and what to serve for dinner on New Year's Day.

Two Schools

Each spouse has lived for about eighteen years in a "school" for marriage, the family of origin—a school without textbooks or lectures (maybe), a school where lessons are learned through daily experience and observation. Children absorb family attitudes about many issues: honesty, race, generosity, hospitality.

Therefore, when two people marry, we have the merger of two schools of thought. Merger or collision. There is the possibility of selectively choosing from each family and respectfully dealing with whatever doesn't fit in this new and unique relationship.

There are potential problems in the fact that each spouse has a clear idea of the right way to deal with each issue, and each one's right way may differ from the other's. This is where compatibility is tested. Literally, compatibility means "suffer together." We can suffer together and struggle through each new issue in a spirit of shared responsibility. Compatibility is not so much a state of affairs as it is the result of negotiation.

We share responsibility for understanding, for listening, for solving problems, for making the marriage a good one.

SHARING

When Rita and I married, we resolved never to fall asleep at night without settling that day's differences between us. However, as time went on, sometimes we were too tired or too angry or both; so, we would make a truce, go to sleep in peace and resolve to thrash it out after work the next day. So far we've been able to keep that agreement.

One morning, after such a late-night truce, I got up early and made the coffee. I left a note by the coffee pot: "I'm sorry for my 10 percent." A little attempt at humor there. When I returned for coffee, there was an addition to the note: "I'm sorry for my 10 percent, too; and when I find the 80 percent rascal, I'll forgive *him*." I've long since forgotten what the spat was about, but I'll never forget the good-willed humor in those notes, an exchange that readied us both for dealing with the issue at the end of that workday.

Seriously, our task is not to fix blame. Our task is rather to fix problems, to find out together how to deal with the issues at hand that concern, affect, involve us both.

We could spend a lot of energy trying to establish who was at fault or how much of the blame belonged to which partner. What a waste! Supposing we could determine precise portions of blame—his, 71.4 percent, hers, 28.6 percent—what good would it do?

What good would come from trying to assign blame if we forget to fix what didn't work? Our job is not to fix blame and punish; rather, how can we move out of this negative situation into a positive solution that profits us both? Two winners, sharing the winnings!

Put it another way: If we could roll back the camera to the beginning of that scene, how could we both rewrite our scripts toward a happier ending?

Roles

It's surprising how many young couples have accepted without thinking the traditional roles on the home front. We need to evaluate our unique situation rather than accept the patterns that may have worked for other couples in other times and in other settings.

Nowadays, it makes sense for a couple to look at what must be done around the house and divide the tasks in an equitable way. The division of labor needs to be renegotiated often as circumstances change—work shifts, sickness, holidays, seasonal tasks.

The goal is: How can we share these tasks in such a way that neither of us feels used, cheated, undervalued? With this goal in mind, how can we take care of all the things that need to be done in such a way that, when all the daily domestic work is done, we both have some energy left over and a good feeling toward each other? There has been no free rider and no martyr.

My own father would not have known which end of a dishtowel to hold. My father was a farmer; my mother was not employed outside the home. Their division of labor worked well for them. Or did it? I remember hearing my mother say, after Papa retired, "*I* haven't retired. My work is the same as it always was, except that he's in the house now." My wife's father was a printer, and his wife was not employed outside the home. They had their own division of labor, a division that is not ours to imitate.

Many couples come to marriage counseling with domestic chore-sharing as an issue. I get their attention when I say solemnly, "Now it is important to understand that certain things are by nature a man's work, and certain things are by nature a woman's work." Then I pause while I watch him smiling in anticipated agreement and she begins to frown.

Then I continue: "And there's an easy way to tell just what is a man's work and what is a woman's work. If it is done with a penis, it's man's work; if it is done with a vagina or nursing breasts, it's clearly woman's work. And everything else is up for grabs."

Then she smiles, and he frowns.

It is rare that any daily chore is gender-related. Maybe the male is physically stronger, but how often do we move the piano?

When either the wife or the husband thinks the sharing is not fair, what is there to do about it? Sit down, look at each other, and talk. And listen. Nagging is surely not the way. Nagging is inefficient. It doesn't work. Nagging is a signal that we're not operating as equals. The alternative is adult-to-adult negotiation, with this understanding: We both want to be fair; neither of us wants to take advantage of the other; we both want to feel like respected partners.

There are several good ways to divvy up domestic duties. Here are some criteria for deciding who does what, for now. These guidelines are to be taken together, not separately.

Who has the time?
Who does it best?
Who is willing to learn?
Who likes to do it?
(I would rather vacuum than dust.)
Who is willing to spare the other?
Who has the energy?
Who has the physical strength?
For whom is the task important?
(Keeping the car clean is low on my priority list.)

My wife once said, "You know, Cranor, you do a lot of work around the house. In fact, some weeks you do more than I do; but I get the impression that you think you're 'helping' me. When I run the vacuum cleaner, it's taken for granted. When you run the vacuum cleaner, I'm supposed to send up a flare." That was a good lesson for me, and I've learned to think in terms of "sharing responsibility," not "helping Rita."

Who Will Do What

There will always be chores nobody likes to do. I have never met the person who relished cleaning the commode. Negotiate. Negotiate as friends and partners. And always repeat the message, internally and aloud, "How can we get all those things done that need to be done today and still have some energy left for each other?"

The goal, I repeat, is to get it done and have time left for ourselves and each other. If the husband does all the housework, the meal planning, the grocery shopping, the cooking, the child care, the dishwashing, and the laundry, is it any wonder he's too tired to make love at 11:00 P.M.?

We can seldom reach total equality in sharing the work load; equality, no; equity, yes. And we renegotiate from time to time. At least every three months, we sit down and talk about how our work sharing is working out now.

In this three-month period, who will write letters to the relatives? Maybe one of you even likes to write; make a rough draft for mutual approval. Who will be responsible for remembering birthdays and anniversaries? Who will call the plumber? Who will complain when the newspaper is not delivered? Who will answer the telephone? Who will answer the doorbell? Must it always be the same person? Must it always be answered?

SHARING

Next to sharing chores, there's the question of sharing dollars. Do we both know how we stand financially? Do we both know how much money is coming in from whatever source? And whose money is it? Do we both know how much is going out, and where? Do we both have a voice? Does each of us have a veto? The one who keeps the books (at present) informs the other, who sits down to listen.

Paying the bills, while never fun, can be time together. One can write the checks and record them while the other takes care of the envelopes and stamps. Even if one does all the bill paying, that one needs to inform the other of their financial condition. And the other must listen. Along with the principle that both of us must know how we stand, there is need, too, to agree to negotiate decisions about what to buy and when, to negotiate any expenditures over a certain amount, depending on a couple's current financial condition. Reaching a consensus is slow but rewarding. Consensus leaves no trail of resentment.

Finally, there must be some amount, again depending on circumstances, that we don't have to account for—pocket money, spending money. We are still individual persons, although we share much. Having to account to each other for every penny is intolerable.

Besides sharing dollars, we share space: closet space, living space, breathing space. In that shared space, no two people have exactly the same standards for cleanliness, for organization, for tidiness, for order. If having coats and hats hanging in their place is important to one, the partner who obliges will be rewarded with thanks. Scattered newspapers may not bother you, but if this is an issue for your spouse, you'll be glad you tidied up because of the thanks you'll receive. Clothes left lying where they fell will irk some people. The appropriate attitude is: Because order is important to this person I love, I'll make the effort. I'll make the effort, not because I exist to please that other person but because that other person's needs matter to me. Let me repeat my example of making the bed (it is so "daily").

If I lived alone, I would never make the bed. Since making the bed is important to my wife, it is something we can do together. And it does look good.

Share: Isn't this one of the first things we teach children as they begin to interact with others? And we're still learning to share as we enter a relationship as important as marriage, learning to share every step of the way, every day. Two relatively independent adults choose to share part of their lives with each other:

—space
—things
—dollars
—time
—energy
—responsibility.

Sharing is a unique tool that brings out the best in both partners and gives the best to each.

EPILOGUE

Can we agree that maintaining a good relationship—and repairing it when necessary—is the hardest work in the world? If we can agree, then take my word for it that it can also be the most rewarding work in the world when two people work together, using good tools well.

Every page of this book is based on the premise that two people want a good marriage. Let's be realistic in a real world. What happens when you don't have a cooperative partner? You can decide if you would be better off alone or with this person. Or, you could give up.

Give up, because when one partner reneges, for good or bad reasons, the marriage can't grow. The best spouse in the county can't maintain and repair a relationship alone.

However, don't presume the other partner doesn't want to try. Check it out. You know that you have good will. Perhaps she or he does too.

Most people want a good relationship. Some are even willing to work for it, if there's hope. This book holds out that hope.

Here you have a kit of ten basic tools for a relationship. That's all. If they make sense to you, try them.

As you use these ten tools, three things will become clear:

- It is difficult to learn to use them well.
- Each tool requires two users, partners working together.
- These tools well used bring a reward that outweighs the effort put into using them, a reward that encourages you to pick them up and try again.

ABOUT THE AUTHOR

In his sixty-six years Cranor F. Graves has observed marriage as a clergyman and then as a marriage and family therapist in private practice, at North Carolina State University Counseling Center, and at a Marine Corps Family Service Center. *Building a Marriage* is the distillation of his work counseling couples.

He lives at Topsail Beach, North Carolina, with his wife, sixty asparagus plants, and a steady stream of wanted guests.